Mexico City Merriness

Rich Hebron

Mexico City Merriness

Rich Hebron

Books by Rich Hebron

Homeless but Human
Primary Ponderings

Nuance & Notes Series

Chicago Clarity
Paris Beauty
New York Energy
Los Angeles Dreams
Miami Magic
Milwaukee Sensibility
Mexico City Merriness
London Happening

Written by Rich Hebron
Illustrated by Kenneth Ferguson

Milly Moves to the Farm
The Boy and the Rocketship

Rich Edition Classics

The Great Gatsby

Rich Hebron is an American author. He has lived half his life in Chicago and the other half on a farm in rural Wisconsin. He fuses these backgrounds together to draw inspiration and live a meaningful life in a world accelerated by the internet and digital technology. He hosts the Rich Conversations Podcast where he explores self-development and talks with friends in art and science fields.

Connect with Rich: @richhebron

For those who want to live with joy

Author's Note

My first near-death experience happened on the farm. An oil line blew on the tractor and became engulfed in flames. I jumped from it. My second near-death experience occurred four years afterwards. This time, three men pointed Uzi guns at my face, threatening to shoot me. Fortunately, it was just another reminder that life will end—all our lives. So how do we want ours to be?

After initially going fast, with the adrenaline from the encounter lasting months, I decided to stop. The difference between speed and velocity is that velocity is speed in a direction. Anyone can go fast—especially in circles. But it takes skill and something deeper to channel energy with purpose. Refining purpose requires restarting at the beginning. Be open and see what's happening. Pursue curiosity and, above all, patience.

My curiosity led me to hotel lobbies. I spent time visiting different ones in downtown Chicago and just sat, observed, and wrote notes, often sipping espresso or red wine. An appreciation for details developed. Gratitude followed. Every thing was there for a reason. Nothing was a coincidence. The creators of the spaces aimed to evoke particular emotions and feelings in people. They staged a vibe.

I learned that design affects our mind and influences our culture. The whole of something is the result of individual things. From a pencil to a house. From a shoe to our cities. From a light fixture to our lives. The story of our life is the result of every individual decision we make. The universe is the result of every individual atom.

Beauty is the result of those small, individual components. Love is understanding those small, individual components.

My passion and appreciation for detail expanded from hotel lobbies to virtually everything in life and in people. But something I especially had fun with was observing the designs on building facades. My favorites were those resembling nature. They possessed the character I aspire to be: dynamic, flexible, playful, and fruitful. Things that are alive are adaptable. Things that are dead are stiff, rigid, and brittle. Since human beings are part of nature, the same is true for people and their ideas and perspectives.

I encourage you to reflect on the follow questions:

- *Are current environments failing to design nuance?*
- *If design affects culture, what are the ramifications of prioritizing cheap and fast?*
- *Is a society that ignores patience a healthy one?*
- *If individuality is abandoned, is Love too?*

This is a series called *Nuance & Notes*.
This is a book of nuance of Mexico City with notes from my mind and observations in the world.

There's a lot going on in Mexico City. It's over-whelming and beautiful. It's crazy in the most positive way. Pride and cheerfulness permeates the culture and a lighthearted nature lives within its people. Love for country and family stands out. Family and friends are loyal. People have permission to tease and joke with one another. Mexico City is a place where the sun smiles, the plants have freedom to stretch, and joy rings throughout.

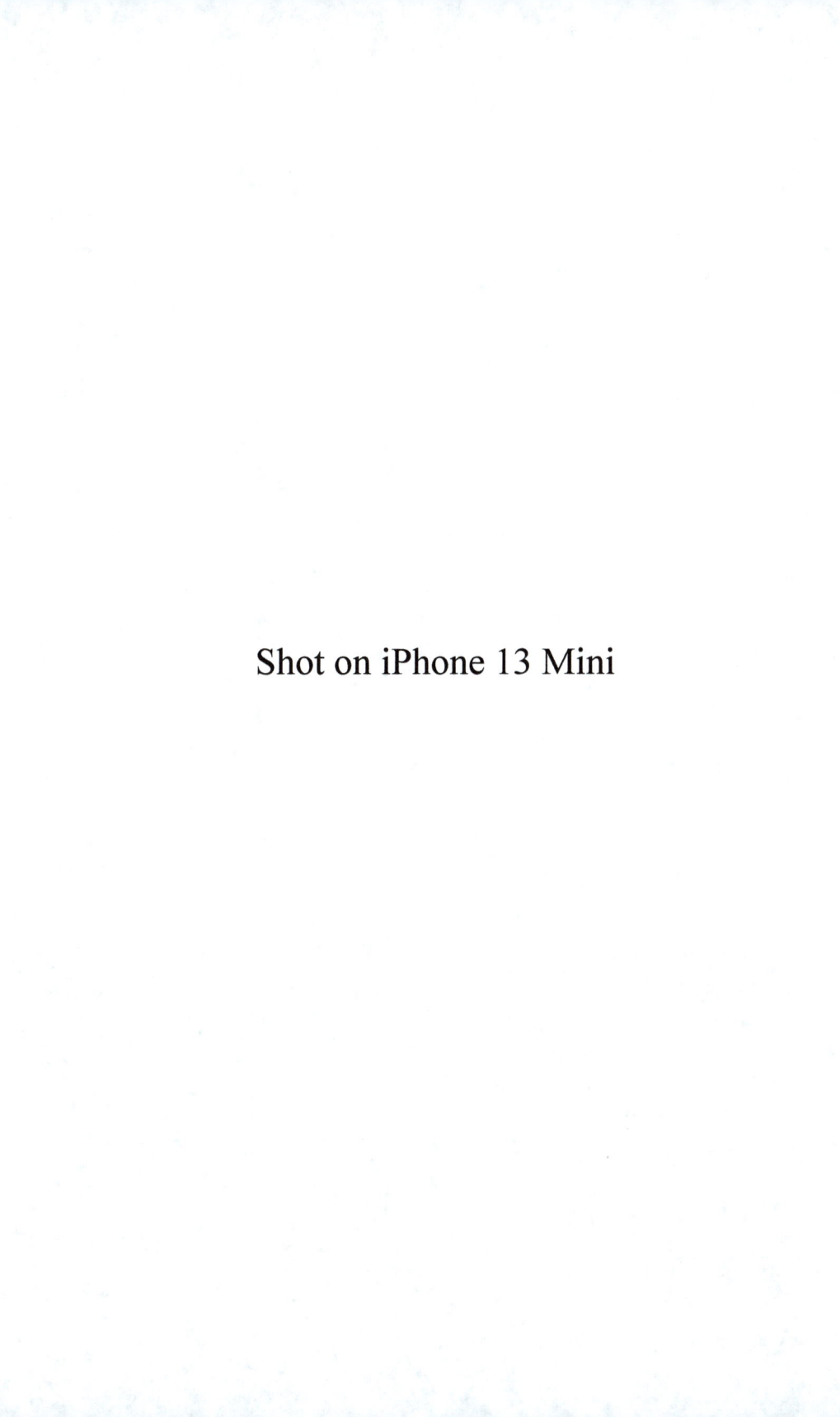

Shot on iPhone 13 Mini

Thanks for the company
so we could be our selves
Kisses

Be prideful of where we are
and where we live

Trees can and will uproot sidewalks

Birds are the chattiest bunch
in the mornings

Follow through is sexy

Everyone gets to where they're going,
so know where we're going

Outstanding espresso
Outstanding day

There are infinite options
Consider it more beautiful than exhausting

Less thinking
More visualizing

The air here is quite a potion
Breathe in its uniqueness

Appreciate a place where people
are unafraid to sing

Rich Hebron

There's no sense of worrying
about tomorrow, today

Every one contributes something

Breakdancing jump ropers at a red light
are treasures of the human experience

Life is lighter with the Sun
and a sense of humor

Rich Hebron

The phenomenal is created through
a curation of sounds and songs

Diversity of skills and talents
is healthy for a community and city

Rich Hebron

More Sun, less anger
More plants, less fear

Lipstick and heels can be as dangerous
as an atomic bomb

A group of people learning
a dance is heartwarming

Celebrate a rich history and culture
It's part of the bigger story

What can the outside teach us?
How can the inside elevate its qualities?

Take a walk and appreciate
the vibrant scenery

The food scene is a tremendous competition
It's a paradise

A lime added to any thing
makes it quite something

Build on top of great
to reach further heights of potential

The connection between the mind and body makes the present amazing

Rich Hebron

It's all about moments,
so live it as close as possible to perfection

Sometimes Darth Vader
hands out flowers

When tired,
remember we never get this night back

Uptight would not be right

Every day is a fiesta baby

Get ready for some hot stuff

Vehicle exhaust, plants, hot air,
and street food create a unique perfume

A violinist playing outside
on a warm Saturday night
is a vibe

Rich Hebron

It's not the perfect who endure
It's those who make perfect of nonperfect

36

The flaky get overlooked within time

Rich Hebron

As ambitious as we can be,
we can only focus on one thing at a time

Calm beats rushed

Breathing reveals degree of health

Sturdy wood furniture has a feel
that plastic or metal don't

Disarm with a smile

Be stellar at curation

That which doesn't stretch, breaks

Buckle up. We're going full throttle

In this moment, what is our focus?

Take rejection like a river
Keep flowing

Some games require playing the numbers
Some games require precision
Be aware of which this is

Think about it
Give it space
It will reveal its self.

Ending gives meaning to the duration

Do not delay
Be happy now

Having friends in other cities is the best

Working together springs miracle waters

Rich Hebron

Travel light so our walk is less sweaty

If it feels like we're trying hard,
it's not right

Important decisions
should feel natural

When people wanna know,
let 'em know

Rich Hebron

A fresh breeze, our favorite music,
and the realization of our dreams

Know before approaching the options,
otherwise they'll overwhelm

Inspire the apathetic through example

Dogs are so happy
And why not?
Smile and stick our tongue out

Rich Hebron

The bleach on the sidewalk
blends with the warm fresh morning air

Cities under the night sky
provide an enchanting magnificence

Balcony views are holistic

The fearlessness of birds is admirable
It earns respect

Rich Hebron

Shared experiences
forrge the deepest bonds

Eat dinner on a garden patio
Be entertained by a rotation
of undiscovered performers and acts

Embrace the ambition and love

An alarm is unnecessary
A woman will call through the streets
for old refridgerators and mattresses

Rich Hebron

Freedom is in a mind,
a laptop, and a passport

Water is important but so is a great attitude

Rich Hebron

Are her earrings
a flower, a pineapple, a dove,
or just heaven?

Love another as real as the love of corn

Life is a bore without risks

Those who look the most harmless
can be the most dangerous

A chorus of thank you's is divine

The common bird
is cute, fearless, and audacious

Rich Hebron

Live life with the spirit
of the most beautiful dress

The moment we've waited for
has waited all this time for us

There are plenty of ways
to connect if we're open to it

Be the most endearing form of a maniac

All day in the sun
and all day without water
isn't wise

A new wave is here
Ride it baby

Rich Hebron

A place with bookstores vibrates

When we're tired, we give in

Rich Hebron

One sip in the shaded sun
takes us to ecstasy

Don't move heaven and earth
only to think the same as all

One moment obscurity
One moment genius

If we want to break free,
breathe and be so

Work on our self
Create high expectations to meet

The moment our mind transcends
is more like a supernova than a light bulb

Don't drag our feet on the sidewalk
or we'll trip on roots

A sense of humor is as fresh and invigorating
as walking on a tree lined street

Rich Hebron

What do we want to do?
There are plenty of options
Pick one and start the adventure

Starting is important
Knowing when to stop is also important

Without decisions comes
inexperience and plateaus

Walkability and happiness
are strongly correlated

If we live with little need,
life will be overflowing
with time and resources

Study the consensus
Be curious of the opposite

Fashion and style reveal thought

There are so many ways
to be generous and kind
Be creative

Be at home
Stay a while

Who sings the loudest?
The birds, the street performers,
or storefront speakers?

A wise person knows
when to be in the sun
and when to be in the shade

Lean into what we fear
Understand it
Embrace it

Rich Hebron

Being one's self
is easy, fresh, and impressive

The movements of ants on a sidewalk
is like humans driving on highways

A simple row of plants
can be the difference
between comedy and tragedy

When we're on a roll,
don't stop and don't apologize

Don't give everything to get nothing
Be nothing to receive everything

Our world changes
the moment we realize we're loved

Rich Hebron

If we understand it all,
we don't understand at all

Appreciate the people and logistics
who helped make it all happen

Dance with somebody,
even if it's our self

Opposite is opportunity

A healthy culture is one that's unafraid
to be together

Are we doing it because
we have to or want to?

Every person collects something,
whether physical or nonphysical

Maximum energy
is found closest to the source

It's easy to live with regrets
Just do what everyone else does
and don't think about it

We've come a long way to get here
Don't forget that
Be grateful

Rich Hebron

Be still and silent
We'll become infinite

Take a little bit more time
to observe the gray
in the black and white

Don't let a culture of complexity
confuse us from the simple

Go outside and create our own entertainment

Appreciate what is fleeting
before it's gone

Practice so much
until it's as easy as breathing

A Thought on Cities

Our cities are our greatest invention. They're the engines of civilization. Cities are the hubs that bring people, ideas, and opportunities together. They generate energy and inspire the pursuit of dreams and a better life.

I feel humans are meant to be isolated in nature or surrounded by other humans. Fusing the two maximizes energy and accelerates regenerative processes. This is why I shuffle between living on a farm in rural America and traveling to big international cities.

Having lived in Chicago for over 15 years, I am an enthusiastic advocate for urban living. I believe that the healthier the city, the more dynamic the society and culture. I'm passionate about exploring and analyzing the facets of each city. I believe in competition and that our cities should be constantly learning, adapting, evolving, and growing to serve and increase the quality of life for its residents. I love observing and comparing cities, noting their strengths and weaknesses, the effects of local geography, the movements and flows, and how every small matter contributes to the larger matter.

Cities are where big things happen. I believed this as a little kid growing up on a farm and I know it now as an adult who has experienced their impact.

I'm proud to combine notes that can help realize individual human potential with artwork that demonstrates the beauty collaboration can produce.

Rich leads weekly self-reflection sessions
to help people live with more joy

Join in on the Rich Conversations Podcast
or visit the Rich Hebron YouTube channel

Connect with Rich: @richhebron

Notes

Notes

Notes

Notes

www.ingramcontent.com/pod-product-compliance
Lightning Source LLC
Chambersburg PA
CBHW071758120626
46550CB00002B/834